Going North!

Tips and Techniques to Advance Yourself

DOMINIQUE B. BRIGHTMON

ISBN: 1539396460
ISBN-13: 978-1539396468

DEDICATION

To my parents David & Ella Brightmon. This book would not have happened without your love, prayers, and words of encouragement. You guys are truly the best in the world. Also to my big brother Wayne Brightmon. You are a true example of brotherly love.

CONTENTS

ACKNOWLEDGMENTS

I want to give a special thanks to all of my mentors, coaches, and friends that helped me with this book. Especially to Shawn Purvis, Daniel Ally, & Dr. Ray Charles.

Also, big thanks to Nick Bush my editor. You made this book come out a lot better than it originally would have.

INTRODUCTION

Has anyone ever asked you "how's it going?" Then would you reply with "fine," "good," or "can't complain?" My response would be "going North!" It's good for comic relief because it takes the question literally. Also, 'going North' goes deeper than that.

When you look at a map and are searching for a location in the North direction, you are going up. Going North is about going up in your life and helping others to get there. North is a philosophy of upward motion: being upbeat and positive, doing more in your life, and helping others to do more as well.

The aim of this book is to take some lessons learned and implemented by others to help you become a better you. Read this book and do something with it! Whether it's taking that 1st step to starting a business or taking more action to fulfill your dreams, let this book assist you on that journey. Some books and messages reach different people at different times for a reason. Let this synthesized package of information be a blessing to you and be the gateway to a much bigger world that awaits you. Be warned. Transformation does not happen overnight, so give it time. Rome wasn't built in a day and big things happen when you're good habits are compounded over time.

The Man Behind the Book

I have over a decade of experience of working with people in a public library setting. This has allowed me to help thousands of people from different walks of life. By helping others you learn how people tick while transforming yourself in the process. Through my transformation, I learned how to connect with more people through public speaking. My passion for public speaking and professional development led me to join Toastmasters International. After joining a local club, I went from being the lowest ranking club officer (Sergeant-At-Arms) to becoming Area Director in two years at the age of 23. This rapid growth came from using the techniques in this book and having a sincere desire to help people.

This book is a result of my passion for reading and helping others. Life advancement is something that everyone desires at one point or another. If you want to advance yourself, be spiritually grounded. No matter what form of spiritual development you choose, have something that fulfills your inner being and strengthens your faith. I'm a born again Christian who was raised in a Baptist church and gained a strong Biblical foundation through extra classes in high school. So there will be some Bible references ahead. Let the life enhancement begin!

1

ADVANCE YOURSELF

"If you want to have more, you have to become more...For things to improve, you have to improve. For things to get better, you have to get better. For things to change, you have to change. When you change, everything changes for you." - Jim Rohn

Going North involves advancing yourself. How do you advance yourself? By taking more action pointed toward the result that you want see. On your journey of upward motion, you must first learn what you want to do. Do you want to become a better speaker, teacher, or writer? This action can be intuitive, but to make it more intentional, use more resources. Libraries are filled with gold, and Google can be your hand held encyclopedia.

The Most Efficient Way to Advance Yourself

If you are going to advance yourself, find a way to do it efficiently. What is the most efficient way to advance yourself in anything you do?

Read books, especially books on the subject you are trying to master. It has been noted that if you read three books on any single subject, you can be considered an expert on that subject. Can you guess why the person who reads only three books is considered an expert? It's because the average person only reads one book per year after finishing their college education.

"I have never let my schooling interfere with my education."
- Mark Twain

Formal education is great, but you can achieve a similar education on your own. If you want to become a better public speaker, then read three or more books on public speaking and practice at your local Toastmasters club. If you want to better manage your time, then pick up a time management book and watch your productivity increase. If you want to become a better leader, then read three books on leadership and implement the strategies that speak to you.

"Leaders are readers." - Charlie Tremendous Jones

Absorbing knowledge from reading is meaningless without implementing what you have learned. One lesson I implemented from my reading was to move slowly through the crowd. Moving slowly through the crowd involves talking to each person you meet and learning their names. This is an important skill to have as a leader because it can lead to opportunities that otherwise would have remain hidden.

When I was attending a conference, a financial adviser greeted me and we talked for a few minutes about Toastmasters since he was wearing a Toastmasters name-tag. During our conversation, he mentioned that there was an open slot for an Area Director. I was excited at the opportunity because it was a chance to enhance my leadership skills at a higher level. After getting me in contact with the appropriate people, I became an Area Director. This would not have happened if "moving slowly through the crowd" hadn't prepared me.

"Knowing is not enough; we must apply. Willing is not enough; we must do."- Johann Wolfgang von Goethe

Reading is the most efficient way to advance yourself, but reading is also another way to help advance others. You may be asking yourself, "How can I advance others through reading?" Well, I'm glad you asked.

When you read books and enhance your problem-solving skills, you can in turn help others to solve their problems.

One morning at the library service desk, a patron came in and told me about his son who was having trouble with Spanish. Naturally, I would have pointed him to the Spanish books. Before I could direct him to the Spanish books, he kept going on about how he's been trying to get his son to become more serious in school. As I listened to him talk for a few minutes, I realized that he not only needed Spanish books but someone to vent to.

After escorting the patron to the Spanish books, I handed him a copy of "My Infamous Life by Prodigy" to give to his son in hopes that he would read it. He was very happy that I took the time to listen. That experience taught me that sometimes people need someone to vent to and that:

"People don't care how much you know until they know how much you care."- John C. Maxwell

Read and advance yourself so that you can help others to advance too. Once you decide on a path, you must take action backed by research. When you study materials written and compiled by those who went before you, you can lessen your learning curve. Since there is nothing new under the sun, there is a massive guarantee that someone out there is doing or has done what you want to do. Seek and find those who have done the things you want to do and mimic the best of them.

Action Items:

1. Ask yourself, *What one skill would I'd like to master by this time next year?*
2. Pick up 3 books on that subject. You can get them from your local library, amazon.com, or a nearby bookstore. Check out the list in the back of this book if you don't know where to start.
3. Record the results from your reading in a notebook or a journal. This allows you to track and measure your progress.

2

R.A.V.E.

"If you want to live on a new level, you have to think on a new level." - John C. Maxwell

Your mind is the greatest computer on the planet because it was made by the Almighty Creator. Allow yourself to be a mini creator. Computers would not exist without the minds and hands of others. Libraries and schools would not exist without the minds and hands of others. Books would not exist without the minds and hands of others.

Going North involves developing and maintaining a mindset of upward mobility. You develop an upward mobility mindset by immersing yourself in optimistic material and surrounding yourself with more positive people. But before you get around more positive people, seek to purge your mind of limiting beliefs (I'm too young, I'm not smart enough, etc.) and feed your mind with uplifting material. Every day we are feeding our minds something, so be selective of what your mind is feasting on. If you watch garbage (the news, reality TV, etc.) then your mind will be filled with garbage. Practice selective ignorance when it comes to placing your eyes and ears around certain things.

R.A.V.E. Method

Rave is defined as talking or writing with extravagant enthusiasm. Once you decide to have a positive mindset, it will lead to boundless enthusiasm. Your enthusiasm will then lead to you speaking and even writing with enthusiasm. With boundless enthusiasm, you will become a walking bundle of fun. When you want to develop a Northern mindset it will involve the following:

- **R**eading (great material).

- **A**udio programs (Listening to them).

- **V**isual stimulation (watching more educational material than entertaining material).

- **E**ncouraging (yourself and others).

Reading

One of the best ways to keep your brain healthy is through reading. You can read an engaging article, or inspirational novel that takes you into another world. Books contain the tools necessary to navigate through life because they contain information that was tested and proven. Here are a few of the many benefits to reading:

- Expanded vocabulary

- Expanded thinking

- Improved memory

- Improved writing ability

- Improved conversational ability

Go into "sponge mode" and absorb as much useful knowledge as possible, then squeeze that onto the planet from your mind, but don't go overboard. Business magnate & American industrialist Andrew Carnegie is noted for saying that "disorganized knowledge is of very little value." Organize your information and implement it. There is a difference between theory and practice. Those who have only theory have invisible and intangible assets. Those who have practiced, have battle tested strength for certain endeavors.

Audio Immersion

When you decide to immerse yourself in audio programs, it can help you get through books easier if you don't like reading (but thanks for reading this book though). Listening to the unabridged audio version of a book can count towards reading the actual book. Make the decision to make your learning mobile, especially if you drive. A study done by the University of Southern California showed that those who drive 12,000 miles a year can acquire the equivalent of a two-year college education in three-years' time by listening to educational audio programs. This means that you can gain more information to add to your mental arsenal.

Audio immersion does not always have to be verbal and educational. It can also be through music. Listening to the ear sugar known as music can boost your productivity. According to author Gary Keller, listening to music while working improves people's mental and emotional states. Music makes listeners feel better about their work, which in turn boosts their mental well-being. This can ultimately create a positive ripple effect that improves other areas of life as well.

Visual Immersion

Reading and listening are great ways to learn but humans also learn through the eyes. This is how sign language is learned and how martial artists transfer techniques to others. Place your eyes upon that which will benefit your mind. Visuals help you enhance your learning ability because the brain is an image processor. The effective use of visuals can decrease learning time, improve comprehension, enhance retrieval, and increase retention.

It has been noted that humans retain visuals quicker and longer than mere words. About 10-20% of words heard from a lecture are remembered after three days. There is a reason why they say that a picture is worth a thousand words.

- The brain can see images that last for just 13 milliseconds.
- Our eyes can register 36,000 visual messages per hour.
- 90% of information transmitted to the brain is visual.
- Visuals are processed 60,000X faster in the brain than text.

This is why company logos like Nike, Starbucks, and McDonald's have no words on their logos. Pointed images hit quicker and stronger than words. Also, don't use this as an excuse for excessive TV time. Your sensory systems are involved in a very limited way when watching television, and you are watching someone else perform interesting or exciting activities. But in the brain, watching another person doing something is no substitute for doing it yourself.

Encouragement

Encouragement will come as a result of what you do with the other three activities. When you work on your inner self to create a better outer world, you will pour out life into others. Japanese researcher and author Masaru Emoto did a study about water and how it can relate to humans regarding the words we speak. In Emoto's book "The Hidden Messages in Water" it shows that humans and water are very much related. Water becomes crystallized over time when positive words are spoken to it. When our vocal power connects and vibrates with water, it will bring about a crystal of light. Water carries vibration, the source of energy. Since our bodies are mostly water, we carry that energy with us. Speak the power of compassion, inspiration, and love into other people's lives.

"How can you tell if someone needs encouragement? That they're still breathing and moving." - Unknown

Through the power of the R.A.V.E. you will see a change over time that will help amplify your life.

Life is a mixture of opportunity and difficulty. Being optimistic can help you when facing danger and going through the inevitable storms of life. Thinking negatively can cause negative results. Always expect the best, do your best, and work for the best.

The RAVE method is built to help you gain a Northern mindset of positivity. Your mind is like a garden and it must be cultivated daily. You must also protect it from weeds and negativity. A garden full of lilies has more splendor than a garden of mushrooms. Protect the garden of your mind by surrounding yourself with more confident and positive people. Guard your mind with your life. You hold the keys to the idea gateway known as your mind.

Keeper of the Keys
By
Guy Gilchrist

You are the Keeper of the Keys.
You are the Guard at The Gate.
Waiting in line to get through that door
Is LOVE. And also HATE.
In line to enter is GENTLE PEACE.
And also VIOLENT WAR.
You must choose who may, and who
May not come through the door.
INTOLERANCE tries to sneak on through
On wings of FEAR, or PRIDE.
It hides behind DREAMS of BELONGING,
And tries to sneak inside.
Oh! Be alert! You're the Guard who decides
Who GOES and who may STAY.
You are The Keeper of The Keys to Your Mind.
Who will you let in today?

Action Items:

1. Listen to and watch more positive, uplifting, and educational material instead of just the news, especially when you first wake up in the morning! If you start your day off with the hypnosis box known as the TV, you'll invite negativity to be your best friend for the rest of the day.
2. Create a productivity and/or hype playlist of your favorite tunes. Listen to this playlist when you wake up to a new day.
3. Compliment or encourage at least 5 people today.

MENTORSHIP: A BOOK ON STEROIDS

"It takes a wise man to learn from his mistakes, but an even wiser man to learn from others." - Zen Proverb

We all have absorbed messages about our group and other groups from culture's throughout our lifetimes. One major way those messages are absorbed, are through mentors. Mentors are those who will assist you in many ways. Whether it's a mentor who shares their experiences with you or a mentor who stretches you. Mentors are a gift.

The Art of Emulation

In my short lifetime, I have had mentors who assisted me in various ways. When I first started working as a part-time library assistant, I was a novice at customer service. My heart for serving people was there, but I needed to learn how to display it.

To become better at my job, I emulated the person who I thought was the best at what he did. After watching some of his actions, and putting my own spin to it, I improved so much that the patrons themselves complimented me on the service they received. Having a mentor at work can help you to improve and develop a sharper focus.

"A good teacher teaches through words. A Great teacher teaches through actions. A good teacher is appreciated. A great teacher is emulated." - Shubha Vilas

Life Advice

During my time in church I wanted to learn more about God, and add more to my bible reading. This led me to joining a Sunday school class. My teacher's name was Mr. J and he was a different type of church leader. He made sure that he was straight up and honest with me. Mr. J taught me a lot but there were two things that stuck with me from his lessons. They were:

1. To know peace, you must know war.

Mr. J would always say that you must be thankful for the good times. When the bad times come, you will be reminded of what the good times were like. If you break your toe and you're stuck limping for a few weeks, you will remember what it was like to walk around normally. When you go through a time that is dark, you will be grateful for the dawn that comes. This also is essential when keeping yourself mentally grounded so that you can battle negativity when it comes. When times are peaceful, you must be thankful. But there will be times when you go through a season of winter where blizzards will block and freeze up your path.

2. The Magic Word "No"

It's good to say yes to opportunities but there is a time where you must say no. Mr. J mentioned to me that when he 1st joined a church during his young adulthood, he said yes to everything. He enjoyed helping the church in any way he could, but he was neglecting his well-being in the process. Because he neglected himself and his health, he had to back away for a while and recuperate. There must be a moment when we all must step back, recollect, and rest. When your energy is not fully dedicated to something, it's better to not be a part of it.

"There's a problem with this life, and it has to do with having so many shiny choices around us that it's easy to fill up our lives with things that aren't essential." - Claire Diaz-Ortiz

When you have had victories in your life, someone most likely cheered you on (even if it had to be yourself). Mentors and coaches have motivated me to become better. When you become better, you can inspire others to become better. Channel the memories of that person who impacted your life in a positive way.

Action Item:

1. If you haven't already, seek someone to mentor you in an area where you want to better yourself. If there is no one in your immediate vicinity that can mentor you, rely on the advice of one of your books to guide you until you get better. Books can be mentors because they were written by people who shared their expertise. On that note, try to contact the author of a book you are reading and learn from them. You can even try to hire them as a coach to help get you further than you would on your own.

4

TIME IS YOUR LIFE'S TRUE BANK ACCOUNT

"Successful, effective people are those who launch directly into their major tasks and then discipline themselves to work steadily and single-mindedly until those tasks are complete." - Brian Tracy

Hourglass Manifesto

Money can be earned back but your time cannot. Energy can be renewed but time cannot. Memories are fleeting and time must expended to get the maximum returns on positive experiences. Life is evanescent. Time is finite and you must focus on completing activities as you move through life. This in essence is priority management and not time management.

In order to manage your time you must first know how much you have. There are 24 hours in a day, and 7 days in a week. Those total 168 hours were given to you and also given to someone else. Your choice of what to do with those hours are your decision alone. Everyone has the same amount of hours, but not everyone maximizes them. In order to keep track of and defend your bank of action known as time, you must be aware of where your priorities lie. Some tasks (and even people) are disguised as time bandits. Know how much time you possess and defend it with your life.

When you love your work, and are not watching the clock while you work, you will lose track of time. Once you lose track of time you will wonder where all the sand disappeared to from your hourglass. This is why people desire time management. God has given us 168 hours in a week to everyone but not everyone maximizes their given time. In the words of Brendon Burchard, "Greatness belongs to those who master their day".

Priority Management

"The older I get the more wisdom I find in the ancient rule of taking first things first. A process which often reduces the most complex human problem to a manageable proportion."
- Dwight D. Eisenhower

Your time goes to where your priorities lie. Make sure each priority is actually a priority. Productivity is priorities realized and goals achieved. Goals are everything! When your goals are met, you can bet on success. Keeping busy with productive activities lead to productive action. Productive action is the cure to the disease known as 'idle time.'

When you want to be productive and creative you must place yourself in the position for creativity to unleash your productivity. A friend of mine once remarked, *some places I can get more work done than in other places.* Find your POP (Place of Productivity).

There are different times throughout the day when you feel a certain way. When it comes to time management, it's really about priority management. In order to have priority management, you must know yourself. When you know yourself and the goals you want to achieve, then you can prioritize effectively. Put to paper your priorities and propel yourself forward. Base your to-do list off of knowing yourself and your priorities.

Manage your time effectively to maximize your performance exponentially. This superpower (or ability) can be gained through priority management. Where your loyalty lies, is where your time is spent. When you have goals to reach and targets to hit you must know where you are going. Because many go forward (or think they are) without knowing where they are going.

Design Your Day with the PAR Method

"Planning is bringing the future into the present so that you can do something about it now." - Alan Lakein

Prepare for the worst. Act on your plans. Reflect on the outcomes. Repeat this process until results happen. In the journey of self-development, I have discovered that those who plot and plan their days get more results. If you plan and get the results after taking the appropriate actions you can reflect and rewind on your progress. Trees take years to grow, and Rome wasn't built in a day.

After preparations are made act on your plan! When action is taken on your plan you can readjust during and after the reflection phase. Use the reflection time as a mirror force moment. Take intel on your actions to see how things worked out. "Did I joke too much? Was my pitch too aggressive?" When you reflect, you open the door of your past to see how history panned out. Did you use a poor tactic or a "war" strategy that backfired from poor implementation. Rewind the film in your mind and see how things worked out.

Design your day to improve your day. How do you design your day? It can be done by visualizing it, making a to-do list, or writing your goals down. It can even be a combination of all three.

Another way to design your day is by asking yourself questions. When you question yourself, you are forcing yourself to think. Questions are powerful tools because they require thought and a response.

Here are five questions that will help you blueprint your day:

Preparation Questions

1. What good will I do today?

Benjamin Franklin asked himself this question daily. Doing good can be as simple as giving someone a compliment or keeping a warm smile on your face. This question is also great for preparing your day to be a positive one.

2. What can I share?

This can be integral to cultivating a sense of gratitude. When your life has been extended for another twenty four hours, you can share some of it with others. You can share some time with family, talent with a company, or treasure with a charitable organization.

3. What must I do?

This question is a powerful one because it forces you to focus on what needs to be done. There could be a book that you want to finish or an important call you need to make. Avoid procrastination by dedicating focused action on what must be done. Procrastination is one of man's most worst traits.

Reflection Questions

4. What good have I done today?

This is the question that you ask yourself when you reflect on your day. Did you accomplish that goal you set for yourself? Did you remain positive and calm through adversity? If you took action on the first question, then you can answer this with ease.

5. What did I learn today?

You must continue to learn if you want to keep growing professionally. Your learning does not always have to be new skills or technical information. It could be as simple as learning that one of your colleagues likes to play video games.

Take the time out to plan and reflect on your day. You are measuring your progress when you plan and reflect. Reflection is introspection. Design your days to design your life.

Preparation + Action + Reflection = A Designed Day

Action Item:

1. Ask yourself the five daily design questions before you go to bed and place your answers on an index card that you keep with you throughout the following day. Refer to the card multiple times daily to stay on course. This allows you to go to bed with a plan in mind for the day ahead.

5

LIFE IS CUSTOMER SERVICE!

"Be a yardstick of quality. Some people aren't used to an environment where excellence is expected." - Steve Jobs

The way you treat people determines your present and future opportunities. If you are familiar with the golden rule, then you understand that people want to be treated like a precious metal. Treasured and important. Treat others the way you want to be treated. Be a person of quality and people will take notice.

"The golden rule is the very foundation of all the better qualities of man." - Napoleon Hill

The Rookie Year Payoff

People may forget your name, but if you made their day, then you'll have a customer for life. Business man & NBA Legend Earvin "Magic" Johnson was making a bid for a building in Los Angeles that would become a multimillion dollar venture. Magic did his research on the majority owner and learned that he was a hard-nosed negotiator who was a stickler about people being on time. When it was time to meet the majority owner, Magic arrived early and won the deal. How did Magic get the deal? It was because the owner's son got an autograph and picture with Magic during his rookie year after he was brushed off by one of Magic's teammates. A kind gesture from the past will pay off future dividends. Never neglect the opportunity to treat a person like a diamond.

"If you take one minute to invest in someone, you will change their whole life." - Dr. Robert Rohn

7 Tips for Excellent Customer Service:

1. See yourself as a world champion performer.

When you see yourself as a world class performer, you will deliver world class service. Visualize yourself at your best and affirm your success. The world is a stage and everyone must play their parts. Play the role of a champion. But don't use this as an excuse to be cocky and arrogant.

2. Project a positive attitude!

When people step into your place of business, they are seeking a fix for their problem(s). Go the extra mile and smile. The world is negative enough already! So help your customers leave with a bit of cheer. Not to mention your positive attitude influences emotion, which influences purchasing decisions.

3. Be aware.

When you are with someone, you must make the impression that you are focused on them. Even if you are present mentally, the person may not believe you are actually paying them any attention. Use eye contact. True listening requires presence and patience. Listening always leads to learning.

4. Seek product mastery.

Focus on the benefits that you offer, and not just the features. A feature is an attribute of the product or useful service. A benefit is the way a service will solve customers' problems. Benefits create emotion.

5. Be content with occasional losses.

Every product or service is not for everybody. You wouldn't go to a dentist to get your computer fixed would you? There are times when you must be content with a loss and recommend someone else as an alternative. Your honesty might even yield return business.

6. Be personable.

Gain an understanding of the customer's state of mind. Ask about their goals, passions, and struggles. Sometimes people do this without asking, and that's when you learn more about them so that you can serve them better. It's knowing what's going on and knowing that you can do great things for people.

7. Make people feel special.

Remember as many names as you can. People love hearing their names more than any other word. Give out compliments. People desire encouragement.

"Everyone has an invisible sign hanging from their neck saying, 'Make me feel important.' Never forget this message when working with people." - Mary Kay Ash

6

ADVANCE YOURSELF PERSONALLY & PROFESSIONALLY THROUGH PUBLIC SPEAKING

Of all the skills that one can possess, public speaking is one that can launch you to a different atmosphere. Public speaking has lead people to many different opportunities. Being able to showcase that you are confident in your verbal communication is a strong asset that will make you a force.

If you want to become better at public speaking, complete this chapter and join your local Toastmasters group to practice. Toastmasters International is a non-profit organization that helps people to develop themselves into better leaders. It has been around for over 90 years and has over 320,000 members worldwide. There are local chapters scattered around the globe for any and everyone who is looking to develop themselves personally and professionally.

Not everyone is meant to be a pro speaker, but everyone can speak like a professional. A professional is organized and can communicate effectively. Being able to verbally express thoughts is crucial to improving the lives of others. Speakers like MLK told us about the dream that lead to change, Malcolm X spoke clearly and is a legendary role model for his effective communication. Great speakers are made through hours of delivery and mastery of language.

5 Reasons Why Speaking More Will Lead to More Personal Growth

1. It helps you to develop more self-confidence.

Public speaking is one of the best ways to develop yourself because it helps you to overcome the top fear known to man (which is public speaking). When you conquer fear at one level it will help you to transcend into another level.

2. It helps you to gain more relationships and connect with more people.

When you are on a platform delivering a message or sharing a story that connects with the audience, you may be invited back to deliver more value. Internalized stories can impact others, especially if they are your own. During one of my talks I mentioned one of my martial arts training stories. After the talk, one of the audience members shared a couple of her Tae Kwon Do experiences with me.

3. It helps you to become a better thinker.

When crafting a speech you will think of what to say and how you want to say it. When you think of what to say, you'll draw out experience from your past that can spice up your presentations.

4. It helps you to gain more knowledge.

When you're going to deliver a presentation, you must research your topic (especially if you don't know too much about it). As you research a topic, you will discover more info or anecdotes that can mesh together to create a winning presentation. Research can lead to reward.

5. It helps you to become a better communicator.

Words are key to communication and communication is key to effective results. The words you use, determine your results in life. If you speak positive reinforcement into others it can build them up. Speak with simplicity. Speak with clarity. When you speak clearly and with simplicity, it will embolden others and bring clarity in other people's lives.

A friend of mine once remarked that public speaking is one of the greatest methods of professional development. This is because you are in front of a group and you are releasing your thoughts to their ears that they may then transfer to paper.

"Your ability to communicate with others will account for fully 85% of your success in your business and in your life." - Brian Tracy

Action Items:

1. When you prepare a speech, practice it. This can be done by doing a dry run from beginning to end. This can also be done by dropping lines from your message in everyday conversation. Avoid Allen Iverson syndrome. Even a little practice is better than none.
2. Join your local Toastmasters club and continue to show up regularly. When you show up, that's the penultimate phase to delivering a message and advancing yourself.

7

FOCUS ALLOWS YOUR LOSSES TO MEAN SOMETHING

"It's hard to be aggressive when you're confused." - Steve Lombardi

When you know your target, you can pierce through any obstacle to get to it. When you are targetless, you will lose momentum because you are shooting in multiple directions instead of a straight shot. When you are focused on a goal, or more importantly your life's purpose and calling, you will be surfing on waves that rise and fall every three seconds. The Bible speaks about not having stability. It mentions in James 1:8 that an unstable man is a double-minded man. Focus on one target with purpose and ferocity to ensure quicker and more favorable success.

Put Life on Pause

There are times when it's best to put things on pause. Life can be a video game because each person has a story to tell, downloadable content to acquire, and a desire to level up. However, you only have one mortal life, no restart button, or phoenix downs to revive your fallen comrades. Pausing can come in many forms. Meditation can be one. In Brian Tracy's books and other programs, he mentions the exercise of sitting still for 60 minutes. I have tried an offshoot of this after listening to Craig Valentine's world championship speech titled the "Key to Fulfillment." The main takeaway from the speech was to sit still and be quiet for 5 minutes. If you become too busy and too excited, your mind will become rough and ragged.

The world is always moving, time is always moving. It can be very detrimental to charge forward recklessly without proper planning, but more importantly without reflection. Reflection is a part of pausing. When you reflect on past victories and lessons learned through non-victories, it can be beneficial your future. The reflected life is the one to have because you examine your past actions to determine how to move forward. Always reflect.

"The unexamined life is not worth living." - Socrates

Do not become so busy in the forest that you never find your way out into the city. Never lose your way if it's working. Just because the Creator made this world, it doesn't mean that we need to drift through life. Don't be a wanderer unless that's your own self-righteous life decision. According to Napoleon Hill, when you drift through life it will cause failure.

Clarity Over Confusion

"If you yourself are deluded, then your surroundings are also a misty, foggy delusion." - Shunryu Suzuki

Lack of focus leads to diminished strength. A half strong warrior is not fit for a full head-on fight. Success in life belongs to the focused individual who is clear on what they want. Clarity comes before everything else. Clarity in thought, religion, action...all things. Clarity gives full sight to what you want to obtain or uphold. Seek oneness with body, mind, and spirit. Clarity in this trinity leads to the completion of a foundation.

When you travel, the bag has to be packed with something. Don't burden yourself with the heavy load of (mental) fog. Strength belongs to those with clarity. Faith belongs to those with clarity. Focus belongs to those with clarity. Victory belongs to those with clarity. Dualism is not pure! Be pure minded by focusing on one thing at a time. Multitasking is mutilating energy by spreading it in multiple directions.

Thinking with clarity is part of seeking missions or goals to meet. You can move relentlessly forward but that forward motion could lead you in the ditch of despair. It is always best to do something that you are sure about but more importantly, something you can learn more about. To think with clarity, you must have the proper information (or intel). The info must be pertinent to the situation you are trying to solve, whether it is changing oil or learning how to communicate better.

Go all in and all out! When you go all in, there is no retreat! When I scattered my focus, my professional life suffered. When you want something you must decide that you really *really* want it, and then you must truly commit to it. After committing to it, implement an all offensive strategy to make it happen. When I did this, I realized that whatever leads to whatever...which isn't much.

Be Intentional

Andrew Carnegie is noted for saying that "disorganized knowledge is of very little value." Organize your information and implement it. As I've said before, There is a difference between theory and practice. Those who have only theory have invisible and intangible assets. Those who have practiced, have battle tested their strength for certain endeavors. Those who combine their found theory with the necessary practice will become an advancing personality and the *ultimate embodiment of success.*

Goal Setting

Do something daily to make your dreams a reality. Make your actions measurable so they can be tracked. Each day is more valuable when you reflect on the value you got out of it. Keep a dry erase board nearby where you can see it daily. Write down your goals for the day, month, or year. Research has shown that people who were happiest were those who were moving closer to achieving their goals. Visible progress leads to visible achievement.

"A better way to stay motivated is by breaking each skill into small manageable tasks." - Peter Voogd

New Year's Mantra

If you have set a new year's resolution before and forgot about it come January 23rd, it's time for a different approach. Starting in 2013, I based each year around a one to three word theme. My word for 2014 was strength. Thanks to the help and encouragement of great coaches, I am now able to perform deadlifts over 300 lbs. When you base your year off of one word, it's easier to remember and allows for more focused action.

Exercise

Exercise has been proven to increase your focus because when your body is moving, it ramps up your mental capacities. There are various exercises that can help you to physically become a better you. Work on the physical to further the mental. Increase physical activities to increase mental capacities. There is an abundance of health books, exercise DVD's and dieting programs for a reason.

Questions Provoke Thought

One of the best ways to focus and create positive momentum in your life is through asking questions. When you question something, it shows that you are curious. When you are curious about something, you will seek to understand it more. When you gain more understanding, you will seek to do things differently or more efficiently.

Questions That Can Focus Your Actions:

1. What do I value the very most in life?
2. What do I want to accomplish?
3. What are my goals?
4. What areas of my life need the most work?
5. Why aren't I already at my goal?
6. What people are most important to me & how much time do I give them?
7. Do I need to forgive someone in my life who needs to be given grace?
8. How do I improve the quality of my work?
9. What is the best use of my time right now?
10. Whom in my life should I take time to thank?

"I never learn anything talking. I only learn things when I ask questions." - Lou Holtz

Action Items:

1. Set some time aside (5 minutes minimum) for sitting down and just being quiet. No music, TV, or any other distractions. For the best results, do this when you first wake up. When you do this for a while, you may extend it to ten, twenty or sixty minutes daily because of the ideas that come and the inner peace that develops. This time is sacred because it clears your mind and opens it up to more ideas.

2. Start exercising more! Head to the gym, CrossFit box, or martial arts school at least twice a week. If that sounds too intense, then do a light set of pushups, situps and squats (don't forget to stretch). If you have a medical condition, seek counsel from your physician for advice first. Whatever you do, just get your body moving more than ever before.

3. Get a piece of paper and write down what you want to accomplish in the next 12 months, and refer to the list constantly throughout the day. Targets are meant to be hit.

8

LEADERSHIP IS ALWAYS IN DEMAND

Leadership is essential during your journey North. When you step out the door of your home you are a leader. This is because people see and people do. When you act, people react. The leadership ability you display is essential once you get to a higher level of your upward journey because leadership ability arrives before a title ever will. Learn to lead and lead well before you are ever given or earned a leadership title. When the time arrives for your arrival, things will come at you fast.

Become Priceless by Seeing the Value in Others

One leadership ability that great leaders have is to see the potential in others. As I was getting started on my Toastmasters journey, I asked a seasoned Toastmaster on how to become a public speaker. One of the things he told me to do was write a book once I got good. A year or so passed by as I delivered better talks, and then I met this lady at a conference. As we were talking, I decided to hand her a copy of my *Dynamic Living Reading List*. When I handed it to her, she looked at the list, then looked at me and asked me where my book was. I was dumbfounded because I never thought of writing a book and publishing it in my 20's. A few months pass by after that conversation and you are now reading a book from a new author because someone saw potential in me and encouraged me to tap into it. Certain individuals are seen as diamonds by some people because God creates people of value. Leaders don't need titles, they just need to positively influence and encourage someone who needs it.

"The greatest good you can do for another is not just to share your riches but to reveal to him his own." - Benjamin Disraeli

Leaders Encourage

Leaders encourage others to think for themselves. A leader must have faith, love, compassion, trust, honesty, and passion. Faith in yourself, your people, and your God. Love for people and your Creator. Compassion for others. Trust in yourself and in others. Honesty with others and yourself. Passion for your mission!

When you are a positive person, your attitude will rub off on others, and they are less likely be negative around you. A leader must have the vision to see the potential in others, and water the seeds of that potential. Because a leader who advances themselves should advance others too. When you advance others the good karma will work in your favor, and you can lessen your chances of isolation. Isolation leads to stagnation.

"A leader is a dealer in hope." - Napoleon Bonaparte

When people feel they have responsibility, they're more likely to take ownership of their job. This applies to life as well. When you decide to be responsible for your life, things change for the better because you take ownership over your mindset, and actions. When you become accountable for your actions, you care a lot more about the results you yield in the future.

Leaders Are Emulated

Leadership also involves being contagious. When you are contagious, you multiply your followers and sphere of influence. In order to be contagious, people have to touch you. How do you get others to touch you? Reach out to them! Whether you are an introvert or extravert, become contagious in your ability to be acknowledged in a room. This can be done by taking initiative in introducing yourself to others. Extend yourself to create trends. Get to know others so others can get to know you.

Leaders Acknowledge People

Being ridiculed is not as damaging as being ignored. This is true because when one feels ignored in multiple areas of life, they will feel more open to disappearing from life (which explains the danger of solitary confinement). When one is ridiculed, they will be damaged but still content thanks to the attention. This is why acknowledging your followers and comrades is essential to being a great leader. Walk slowly through the crowd and acknowledge the gems in the room known as your followers (or colleagues). Make them feel like a crisp $100 bill and your influence will become a force of nature.

Leadership grows out of taking action based on your own free will. Leaders take action. Successful men take action and people who take action are leaders. *Initiative is the gateway to leadership.*

Leaders Are Listeners

Good ears are among a leader's most important features. True listening requires presence and patience. Listening always leads to learning. Whether it's learning about a new opportunity or that you need to get far away from certain people. Leaders value their business (personal and public) by using their ears.

Leaders are Mission Focused

In Colossians 3:2, it says that one should keep their mind on the things that are of Christ. Christ is a great example of living. His leadership was shown through His actions, His disciples, and the magnificent qualities that all people should strive to have, like patience. It takes patience to lead a rag tag group of men who come from different circles of life. Another quality was resilience. Resilience to all negative forces. Whether it was dealing with the Pharisee's, or resigning to His fate to be the perfect sin sacrifice for man, Christ was a focused man who discovered his mission, stuck to it, and succeeded.

9

DECIDE TO KEEP GOING!

Desire For Change

"You cannot change the seasons but you can change yourself."
- Jim Rohn

If you desire change, you must take initiative! Know thyself. Lead thyself. Allow the Creator to work his wonder of serendipity in your life once you move. Momentum starts with movement. To move North, there will be moments when things go south. Take the initiative to move from your valley to victory!

In the summer of 2012 my father went out for a drive and never came back home. Our family went out looking for him and thanks to some help from the police, they were able to find him and get him checked into a hospital. It was good to know where my dad was and it was great to know that he had no injuries. However, we discovered that he had Alzheimer's.

After finding out that he was diagnosed with the evil disease, he was no longer allowed to drive. That led to me doing more to assist around the home. On the day of my 21st birthday, I crashed my car while driving in the rain. Even though I walked out with no injuries, there was still an internal injury that needed healing.

One thing led to another and I almost lost my job because of my poor performance. I needed to shape up because of my back to back screw ups, and I had to change somehow. If there was a solution it had to be in the information sanctuary known as the library, and thus my reinvention process began.

I picked up some books and audio programs that have helped me to amplify my life and make a dynamic decision to improve myself and become better. My desire for change, led to job promotions, a new mindset, and a deeper sense of spiritual identity.

Incomplete Yet Immaculate

"When you aim for perfection you discover it's a moving target." - George Fisher

My final challenge to you is to find the immaculate within the incomplete. Find perfect existence through imperfect existence. This is being "incomplete yet immaculate," being happy in the journey of continuous improvement. We are imperfect beings created by a perfect creator who will allow us to reach a higher level. Go North with the thought of never ceasing to improve and always getting better with time.

You become better by helping others to become better. Zig Ziglar was famously known for saying "you can have everything in life you want, if you help enough other people get what they want." Advance others to advance yourself. The climb to the top will be lined up with obstacles and people that will challenge you to grow. When you're blessed, bless others. Strength comes from within when you start to move. Go North!

Each and every person was created for a distinct purpose. Whether it is to inspire people through speaking, building homes for others, or being that mother who is their child's biggest fan. Your success is something that blooms once you release the thoughts of gloom and doom. Never let others or your mind become a petri dish of negativity. Now is the time to keep going north. This book is one of many that are out there right now and there is one in particular that must be acknowledged. The living book known as you.

"Your life is like a book. The title page is your name, the preface your introduction to the world. The pages are a daily record of your efforts, trials, pleasures, discouragements, and achievements. Day by day your thoughts and acts are being inscribed in your book of life. Hour by hour, the record is being made that must stand for all time. Once the word finis must be written, let it then be said of your book that it is a record of noble purpose, generous service, and work well-done." - Grenville Kleiser

References:

- https://www.psychologytoday.com/blog/get-psyched/201207/learning-through-visuals
- http://info.shiftelearning.com/blog/bid/350326/Studies-Confirm-the-Power-of-Visuals-in-eLearning
- http://www.lifehack.org/articles/lifestyle/10-benefits-reading-why-you-should-read-everyday.html
- http://www.the1thing.com/blog/the-one-thing/fine-tune-your-productivity-with-music/
- The Hidden Messages in Water by Masaru Emoto
- Keep Your Brain Alive by Lawrence C. Katz & Manning Rubin
- 32 Ways to Be a Champion in Business by Earvin "Magic" Johnson
- 100 Simple Secrets of Happy People by David Niven

100 Books for Dynamic Living

1. The Holy Bible

2. Striking Wisdom by Bruce Lee & James Little

3. Ten Ancient Scrolls For Success by OG Mandino

4. The 21 Indispensable Qualities of a Leader by John C. Maxwell

5. Thinking For a Change by John C. Maxwell

6. The Art of War by Sun Tzu

7. The Richest Man Who Ever Lived by Steven K. Scott

8. The Alchemist by Paulo Coelho

9. As a Man Thinketh by James Allen

10. Verbal Judo by George Thompson

11. You Are the Boss by Daniel A. Ally

12. Get Paid & Promoted Faster by Brian Tracy

13. Victory Over Vice by Fulton J. Sheen

14. Who Moved My Cheese by Spencer Johnson

15. The Top 10 Distinctions Between Millionaires & The Middle Class by Keith Cameron Smith

16. The Four Agreements by Don Miguel Ruiz

17. Conversation by Theodore Zeldin

18. Warrior of the Light by Paulo Coelho

19. Checkmate: The 16 Rules of Leadership by Secret Entourage

20. Failing Forward by John C. Maxwell

21. The Small Talk Handbook by Melissa Wadsworth

22. The Top 10 Distinctions Between Entrepreneurs & Employees by Keith Cameron Smith

23. Leadership Secrets of Attila the Hun by Wess Roberts

24. Secrets of the Millionaire Mind by T. Harv Eker

25. Acres of Diamonds by Russell Herman Conwell

26. The Magic of Thinking Big by David Schwartz

27. The Way to Wealth by Benjamin Franklin

28. The Greatest Mystery in the World by Og Mandino

29. 100 Ways to Motivate Others by Steve Chandler

30. Improv Wisdom by Patricia Ryan Madson

31. In Tune With The Infinite by Ralph Waldo Trine

32. The Magic of Getting What You Want by David Schwartz

33. The One Thing by Gary Keller

34. Competitive Leadership: Twelve principles for Success by Brian Billick

35. Outwitting the Devil by Napoleon Hill & Sharon Lechter

36. The Journey from Success to Significance by John C. Maxwell

37. The 17 Essential Qualities of a Team Player by John Maxwell

38. Rich Dad, Poor Dad by Robert T. Kiyosaki

39. Speaker, Leader, Champion by Jeremy Donovan & Ron Avery

40. Display of Power by Daymond John

41. The Tao of Wu by The RZA

42. The 21 Irrefutable Laws of Leadership Tested by Time: Those Who Followed Them...and Those Who Didn't! By James Garlow

43. Summit: Reach Your Peak and Elevate Your Customers' Experience by F. Scott Addis

44. You Don't Need a Title to Be a Leader: How Anyone, Anywhere, Can Make a Positive Difference by Mark Sanborn

45. The Science of Getting Rich by Wallace D. Wattles

46. Straight A's Never Made Anybody Rich by Wess Roberts

47. The Education of Millionaires by Michael Ellsberg

48. The 48 Laws of Power by Robert Greene

49. The Seven Laws of Spiritual Success by Deepak Chopra

50. The Book of Five Rings by Musashi Miyamoto

51. Eat That Frog! By Brian Tracy

52. Soul of the Samurai by Thomas Cleary

53. The Power of Charm by Brian Tracy & Ron Arden

54. Talk Like TED by Carmine Gallo

55. Man's Search for Meaning by Viktor Frankl

56. The Richest Man in Babylon by George Clason

57. Mindset: The New Psychology of Achievement by Carol Dweck

58. Think & Grow Rich by Napoleon Hill

59. The Apocrypha

60. The Greatest Man Who Ever Lived by Steven K. Scott

61. My Utmost for His Highest by Oswald Chambers

62. The War of Art by Steven Pressfield

63. The Master Key System by Charles Haanel

64. Lies My Teacher Told Me by James W. Loewen

65. Covert Persuasion by Kevin Hogan

66. 177 Mental Toughness Secrets of the World Class by Steve Siebold

67. The Autobiography of Malcolm X

68. Maximum Achievement by Brian Tracy

69. Winning With People by John Maxwell

70. Conspiracy of the Rich by Robert T. Kiyosaki

71. The Power of the Subconscious Mind by Joseph Murphy

72. Enchantment by Guy Kawasaki

73. The Rules of Life by Richard Templar

74. Mastery by George Leonard

75. The Treasury of Quotes by Jim Rohn

76. The Five Major Pieces to the Life Puzzle by Jim Rohn

77. Gold Nuggets by Osho

78. Something Else to Smile About by Zig Ziglar

79. The Wisdom of Andrew Carnegie As Told to Napoleon Hill

80. The Prince by Niccolo Machiavelli

81. How to Get Control of Your Time & Your Life by Alan Lakein

82. The 10X Rule by Grant Cardone

83. If Ignorance Is Bliss, Why Aren't There More Happy People? By John Lloyd & John Mitchinson

84. How Successful People Grow by John C. Maxwell

85. Win the Crowd by Steve Cohen

86. The 21 Irrefutable Laws of Leadership by John C. Maxwell

87. How to Win Friends & Influence People by Dale Carnegie

88. The Undefeated Mind by Alex Lickerman

89. Jewish Wisdom for Business Success by Levi Brackman

90. The Compound Effect by Darren Hardy

91. The Better Life by Claire Diaz-Ortiz

92. Influence by Robert Cialdini

93. The Wisdom of Generations by Tieman Dippel Jr.

94. Ultimate Speed Reading by Arthur A. Bell

95. Negotiation by Brian Tracy

96. Mastery by Robert Greene

97. The Art of Stillness by Pico Iyer

98. How Rich People Think by Steve Siebold

99. One Small Step Can Change Your Life: The Kaizen Way by Robert Maurer

100. The Greatest Minds and Ideas of All Time by Will Durant

GOING NORTH!

Top 15 Audio Programs

1. The Strangest Secret by Earl Nightingale

2. The Rules of Success by Grant Cardone

3. The Ultimate Goal System by Brian Tracy

4. How Successful People Win by John Maxwell

5. Greatness is Upon You by Dr. Eric Thomas

6. Born to Win by Tom & Zig Ziglar

7. Little Green Book of Getting Your Way by Jeffrey Gitomer

8. The Little Book of Talent by Daniel Coyle

9. Stand & Deliver by Dale Carnegie

10. Think & Grow Rich: A Black Choice by Dennis Kimbro

11. The 33 Strategies of War by Robert Greene

12. Selling You by Napoleon Hill

13. Destiny by TD Jakes

14. The Success Principles by Jack Canfield

15. Unleash the Power Within by Anthony Robbins

ABOUT THE AUTHOR

Dominique Brightmon is an avid reader and award winning speaker. He is an active member of Toastmasters International and has been awarded for his leadership in 2015-2016 as an Area Director. He currently resides in Baltimore, Maryland where he works as a librarian.

Facebook: Dom Brightmon
Twitter: @DomBrightmon
Linked-In: dombrightmon
YouTube: Dom Brightmon

CPSIA information can be obtained
at www.ICGtesting.com
Printed in the USA
LVHW021842220719
624877LV00012B/157